Chase Me Up Farndale /
s'il vous plaît!

A comedy

David McGillivray and Walter Zerlin Jnr

Samuel French — London
New York - Toronto - Hollywood

FOR AMATEUR PRODUCTION ENQUIRIES

UNITED KINGDOM AND WORLD
EXCLUDING NORTH AMERICA

plays@SamuelFrench-London.co.uk

020 7255 4302/01

Each title is subject to availability from Samuel French,

depending upon country of performance.

Other plays by
David McGillivray and Walter Zerlin Jnr
published by Samuel French Ltd

The Farndale Avenue Housing Estate
Townswomen's Guild Dramatic Society
Murder Mystery

The Farndale Avenue Housing Estate
Townswomen's Guild Dramatic Society's
Production of *A Christmas Carol*

The Farndale Avenue Housing Estate
Townswomen's Guild Dramatic Society's
Production of *Macbeth*

The Farndale Avenue Housing Estate
Townswomen's Guild Operatic Society's
Production of *The Mikado*

The Haunted Through Lounge and Recessed Dining Nook
at Farndale Castle

They Came from Mars and Landed Outside the Farndale Avenue
Church Hall in Time for
the Townswomen's Guild's Coffee Morning

We Found Love and an Exquisite Set of Porcelain Figurines Aboard
the SS *Farndale Avenue*

CHASE ME UP FARNDALE AVENUE, S'IL VOUS PLAIT!

The original version was first presented on 16th August, 1982 at the Edinburgh Festival Fringe. This revised version was first presented at the Palace Theatre, Newark, on 2nd March, 1993, with the following cast of characters:

Mrs Reece   Norma Howard
   (playing Frank and Mary Carrott;
    an Animal)
Thelma   Teresa Selfe
   (playing Brigitte Charot; Jack and
    Norah Garrett)
Felicity   Anna MacNeil
   (playing Constance Barrett; Fifi and
    Jojo)
Minnie   Debby Holden
   (playing Roger Parrot; Jacques Charot)
Gordon   Robert Joyce
   (playing George Barrett; Virginia Parrot)

Directed by David McGillivray
Designed by Gerald Tagg and Walter Zerlin Jnr

CHARACTERS

Mrs Reece: elegant, bossy, enterprising; 50s.

Thelma: quick-tempered prima donna; late 40s.

Felicity: nervous, well-meaning but incompetent actress; late 20s.

Minnie: scatty, good-natured, tubby; not young.

Gordon: long-suffering stage manager, frozen-faced and monotonous when acting; age immaterial.

AUTHORS' NOTE

Chase Me Up Farndale Avenue, s' il vous plaît! was the fourth in the Farndale Ladies' cycle. The original production of the play toured Britain in 1982 with a cast including Julian Clary as Mrs Reece, Deborah Klein (later half of the cabaret act Parker and Klein) as Thelma, and David McGillivray, who introduced the character of Gordon. At one point Thelma exclaims: "Quelle surprise!", which later became Julian's catch-phrase. For the revised version, we made several amendments, notably the addition of Thelma's stirring rendition of the French national anthem, and the Ladies' climactic cancan. Regrettably the plot is no easier to follow.

David McGillivray
Walter Zerlin Jnr
London, June 1993

PROLOGUE

The set represents two adjoining rooms in a small apartment house in the Champs-Elysées. It is a summer morning

There is a single bed in the room L. *Also in this room is a door (A)* UC, *and a painted window* L *showing a view of the Arc de Triomphe. Downstage of the window is a table with a record-player on it*

In the room R *there are two doors* UC; *one (B) is upside-down, that next to it (C) is normal. There is a fourth door (D)* DR *with a practical handle on the hinged side. Upstage of this door is a tall, narrow cupboard. There are also two small tables; one is* DC, *the other — containing drinks, glasses and a telephone — is* DR. *There are upright chairs in both rooms. Paint and wallpaper are different in each room. Stage lights are to half*

The House Lights are up. A selection from Offenbach's Orpheus in the Underworld *is playing as the audience enters. They are greeted by the Chairman of the Dramatic Society, Mrs Reece, and her second-in-command, Thelma, who carry tricolours*

When most of the audience is seated, Felicity enters through door D as Fifi the maid. She carries a Hoover, which she plugs in and begins pushing round. Sound effect of a Hoover, which makes Mrs Reece look at the stage in surprise. Sound effect of the telephone ringing. Fifi switches off the Hoover and the noise stops. Fifi picks up the telephone receiver

Fifi 'Allo! Ici les Chambres du Oo-la-la, an apartment 'ouse...

Mrs Reece clears her throat very loudly. When Fifi breaks off, Mrs Reece shakes her head at her. Fifi looks perplexed. Mrs Reece makes shooing motions with her hand

But Minnie said to come on.
Mrs Reece There might be a few more people yet, dear.
Fifi Minnie said there wouldn't be any more.
Mrs Reece Yes, but there might. Now go away.
Fifi But Minnie said to come on early because you wanted to catch the end of [*programme showing on television tonight*].

Mrs Reece Look, if Minnie told you to put your hand in the fire, would you do that?

Fifi But she's been organizing everything.

Mrs Reece Oh, has she now? Well, perhaps you'd like to tell her that I'm the Chairman of the Society, thank you very much. Now just go back in the wings and *I'll* tell you when we're ready.

Fifi What will you say?

Mrs Reece I'll tell you to come on.

Fifi Yes, but will you use those actual words?

Mrs Reece Yes, I'll say "Come on now". All right?

This seems to satisfy Fifi, who takes the Hoover and exits through door D

Mrs Reece (*to Thelma*) Terribly keen!

Thelma That girl shouldn't be acting.

Mrs Reece But she has such enthusiasm, Thelma.

Thelma She can be enthusiastic backstage.

Mrs Reece Not so loudly, dear.

Thelma Why can't she help Joyce with the sound?

Mrs Reece Because she shows great promise as a performer.

Thelma Oh, come on, Phoebe.

Mrs Reece It's true.

Thelma Come on now!

Fifi dutifully enters through door D with the Hoover, which she plugs in

Mrs Reece You're forgetting how delightful she was as one of the witches in *Macbeth*.

Thelma She came on early in that as well.

Mrs Reece No, she didn't.

Thelma Yes, she did. She came on in the dagger scene.

Mrs Reece Only fleetingly.

Fifi switches on the Hoover. Sound effect of the Hoover. Sound effect of the telephone. Fifi switches off the Hoover and picks up the telephone receiver

Fifi 'Allo! Ici les Chambres du Oo-la-la, an apartment 'ouse ——

Mrs Reece (*interrupting*) Felicity! Not yet, Felicity!

Fifi But you said it.

Mrs Reece Joyce, will you turn that tape recorder off?

The Hoover noise stops

Joyce (*off*) Aren't we starting?

Mrs Reece Felicity, can I have a word with you, dear? If you really think it's a good idea to do the play with the rest of the cast still drinking tea in the dressing-room, well, all right, we'll give it a try.

Fifi No, I don't want to do that, Mrs Reece.

Mrs Reece You don't? You don't want to do a one-woman show?

Fifi No.

Mrs Reece In that case I'll tell you when we're ready.

Fifi You'll be sure to tell me, will you?

Mrs Reece Yes, dear, I'll be sure to tell you. I know, we'll have a code, shall we? What shall we have? I'll say...ooh...*The Sound of Music*, and then you come on.

Fifi *The Sound of Music.*

Mrs Reece Yes.

Fifi turns to leave

Don't forget your Hoover, dear.

Fifi takes it and exits through door D

The House Lights go down. Mrs Reece mounts the stage

Well, good-evening, ladies and gentlemen, and to our honoured guests from France I'd like to say "Bonsoir, mesdames et monsieurs et bienvenue en [*name of town*]."

Audience Bonsoir!

Mrs Reece Voulez-vous me joindre dans l'interval pour une tasse de thé et un ginger nut, s'il vous plaît? Bon!

Gordon appears at an auditorium door and argues noisily with Thelma

Mrs Reece For those of you who are unaware, [*name of town*] has been twinned with [*same name of town*]-sur-Mer in the south of France. Members of the [*same name of town*]-sur-Mer Dramatic Society are with us tonight for our French-flavoured evening. Ssshh! And Thelma and I will be returning the compliment when we visit the French Riviera next month. I don't know if it's of any interest, but I found this wonderful new sun tan lotion, which...Gordon, what is it?

Gordon Thelma's taken my ——

Mrs Reece Not while I'm talking.

Gordon But she's taken my eyeliner.

Mrs Reece Not now.

Gordon You can't leave anything lying around this place.

Gordon exits, grumbling

Mrs Reece Good old Gordon. He's in a bit of a flap because tonight he's not only our stage manager. He's also going to be doing some acting! Good news for everyone who saw him last year as Beth in *Little Women*. I can see our French guests are looking a little puzzled now! It's probably not the case in France, but in this country ladies such as us sometimes have male members. So there's something you can put on your postcards! Now tonight, as I say, we're off on a fun-packed trip to gay Paree. But this isn't the first time the Society has gone Continental. Older members will recall with pleasure such lovely plays as Good Night Vienna, Toodle-Pip Bratislava and Cavey Girls! It's Fräulein Humperdink. And recently we have been exercising hitherto untried skills as we ventured forth into the musical. Music-lovers will have cause to remember Naughty Marietta, The Student Prince and...er...I seem to have lost the next page. What was that other musical we did? Famous one. With all the nuns. Set in Austria.
Audience *The Sound of Music.*
Mrs Reece The what?
Audience *The Sound of Music.*

Fifi enters through door D with the Hoover and plugs it in

Mrs Reece No, not that one. Oh, I remember: Gay Nuns of Salzburg. I was a nun in that. I was *the* nun in that. You were a nun as well, weren't you, Thelma?
Thelma No.
Mrs Reece What were you?
Thelma A yodelling burgomaster.

Fifi switches on the Hoover. Sound effect is heard. Turning, Mrs Reece glares icily at Fifi until she notices

Fifi seems to be on the point of tears as she runs out through door D

Mrs Reece (*shouting over noise of the Hoover*) I think one or two of our younger members are a little over-excited by our gala evening. And by the sound of it our tape recorder's playing up again. Joyce, are you having trouble, dear? Can you give her a hand, Malcolm? We're being Hoovered to death down here.

Sound effect stops

Ah, success. That's Joyce as always on the tape recorder. And she's up there with Malcolm, that's Thelma's husband, who's switching the lights on and off for us. They really have been working like demons. Last week they were in that little box together every night until I don't know when ——
Thelma Not last week, Phoebe. We didn't have rehearsals last week.
Mrs Reece Yes, but they did. I saw them.
Thelma Last week? But ... Malcolm told me he was greasing his pistons...
Mrs Reece Well, I'm not one to gossip. Anyway, keep up the good work, you two. And now let's settle back for a good laugh.

Mrs Reece and Thelma exit through door C. Mrs Reece enters

We present *Chase Me Up Farndale Avenue, s'il vous plaît!* Thank you.

She exits uncertainly

A burst of Hoover noise, which cuts off abruptly

Mrs Reece (*off*) Felicity! Felicity!
Fifi (*off*) What?
Mrs Reece (*off*) We're ready!
Fifi (*off*) You didn't say it.
Mrs Reece (*off*) Felicity! Everybody's waiting.

Mrs Reece puts her head round the door

I'm sorry, ladies and gentlemen. Je suis très désolé.

She disappears again

Fifi (*off*) You were going to say *The Sound of Music*. You *told* me you were going to say ——
Mrs Reece (*off*) Felicity, this is ridiculous. There's an empty stage out there ——
Fifi (*off*) You must say *The Sound of Music*.
Mrs Reece (*off*) All right! *The Sound of Music*! There, said it, made you happy?
Fifi (*off*) Some people in this society are so amateurish.

She strides angrily through door D and grabs the Hoover

She simmers for a moment then goes R and kicks the socket. There is a flash. Fifi jumps back with a scream and clutches her leg

When it is apparent that she is not going to continue, Mrs Reece's arms, making beckoning movements, appear from door D

Mrs Reece (*off*) Come off! Come off, dear!
Fifi I've been burnt! I can't walk!

Mrs Reece edges on, helping Fifi off

Mrs Reece Give me your hand. Everything's going to be all right. Gordon, go and get some butter, will you?

Much commotion off as Fifi is helped through the door

(*To the audience*) We've had a minor accident, ladies and gentlemen. I'm afraid our electrician has a little difficulty with plugs. He's colour blind. but we'll be starting again in a minute...
Gordon (*off*) We haven't got any butter, Mrs Reece.
Mrs Reece There's some [*brand of margarine*] on Joyce's sandwiches. Can you scrape it off?
Gordon (*off*) Joyce!
Mrs Reece Don't use the fish paste ones. She'll end up smelling like a pilchard.

She hurries out of door D. During the ensuing dialogue, she can be seen through the open door trying to get Fifi on to her feet

Fifi (*off*) Aaahhh!
Mrs Reece (*off*) Felicity, dear, you can't lie here. This is an exit.
Fifi (*off*) But it's the stabbing pain, Mrs Reece.

Mrs Reece appears

Mrs Reece (*to the audience*) I suppose the orthopaedic surgeon didn't come tonight, did he? No, too much to expect.
Fifi (*off*) Mrs Reece!
Mrs Reece I'm here, dear.

Mrs Reece disappears

(*Off*) Minnie, give me a hand. This leg has got to go higher than her head.
Minnie (*off*) No, no, no, Mrs Reece. Her head's got to go between her knees.
Mrs Reece (*off*) But not backwards, dear, surely? Come on let's get her on her feet. One, two, three...

Crash and groan off

(*Off*) Butterfingers.

Gordon bursts in through door C with a plate of sandwiches

Gordon I've found Joyce's sandw —— (*He is horrified when he sees the audience*) Oh, my God. This is the stage ...

Thelma appears in the doorway behind him. She holds a stick of make-up

Thelma Here's your bloody eyeliner. It was in your toilet bag.
Gordon I said I didn't want anyone going through my private toilet bag!
Thelma Don't worry, I won't touch the smelly old thing again.

This argument continues as Gordon edges out of door C. Mrs Reece enters through door D, crosses swiftly to door C and closes it on the disturbance

Mrs Reece Now in a way I'm glad we've stopped, ladies and gentlemen, because it gives me an opportunity to draw your attention to an alteration in the programme. The parts of Roger Parrot and Jacques Charot will not be played by Verity Wheatcroft. Many of you will know that Verity is no longer with us due to a difference of opinion. And I don't want to add any more than that. Except to say that no-one could accuse us of being mean with the chocolate digestives. But luckily Minnie Robinson, who's one of Mrs Cav's team in Wardrobe, has stepped into the breach, and I know she's going to be an absolute scream. Although, of course, she will be reading from the script. So bear with us. (*Into the wings*) Is the patient approaching recovery? Yes? Oh, splendid. (*To the audience*) Nous commence!

She backs through door D

The Lights L fade to Black-out

ACT I

The Lights R *come up to full*

Fifi (*off*) I can't find the Hoover!

*More consternation backstage: running feet, cries of "Who's moved it?",
etc.*

Thelma opens door C, looks directly at the vacuum cleaner

Thelma (*as she goes*) It's not here.

Thelma exits

Mrs Reece (*off*) Go on without it!
Fifi (*off*) I can't!
Mrs Reece (*off*) Mime it!

*Fifi enters through door D, whining, with her leg bandaged. She sees the
vacuum cleaner*

Fifi (*calling off*) It was here all the time. Sorry.

*Groans backstage. Fifi limps over to the vacuum cleaner. She switches it on
and begins manoeuvring it but there is no sound effect. This is heard some
moments later. Then the telephone rings. Fifi switches off the vacuum
cleaner, but the sound continues. Fifi limps uncertainly to the telephone and
picks up the receiver*

'Allo! Ici les Chambres du Oo-la-la, an apartment 'ouse ... er ... one
moment, s'il vous plaît. (*Shouting*) I will turn down ze 'oovair.

*She takes a step towards the vacuum cleaner, but the noise stops. She returns
to the telephone*

Ici les Chambres du Oo-la-la, an apartment 'ouse in ze Champs-Elysées
populair wiz Englishmen spending business weekends in Paris. Je suis Fifi
ze maid. 'Oo iz zat? Mais oui, Madame Barrett, I will give your 'usband

a message avec plaisir. You 'ave decided to join 'im 'ere in Paris and will
arrive at four o'clock. Bon. Merci. Au revoir. Ah, non! Wait, wait, wait!
Did you say you were Madame Barrett, wife of ze Englishman 'ere in room
twenty-three, or Madame Parrot, wife of ze ozair Englishman next door in
room twenty-four? Oh, sacrebleu. She is gone. (*She hangs up*) Ah, Barrett,
Parrot — it is so confusing for Fifi. I sink she say "Parrot". I will write
Monsieur Parrot a note.

*She picks up a notepad and pencil, which breaks. She is wondering what to
do when Gordon hands a second pencil from the wings* DR

Gordon (*off*) Psst!

Fifi quickly takes the pencil, which breaks

Fifi Encore, s'il vous plaît.
Gordon (*off*) There's no more.

Pause

Fifi Non, I will not write a note. (*She throws the pad away*) I will ... send a
telegram. (*She picks up the telephone*) 'Allo, telegrams? Please tell
Monsieur Parrot zat 'is wife will join 'im 'ere at four o'clock. Merci
beaucoup. (*She hangs up*) And now I must do ze dusting.

*She pulls out a duster, but the vacuum cleaner effect is heard. Fifi replaces
the duster*

I will do ze dusting wiz ze 'oovair.

*She Hoovers, bending down very low and looking anxiously over her
shoulder at door D*

*After some scuffling Minnie is pushed through it. She is dressed in male
attire as Roger Parrot, but has forgotten to take her pincushion off her
wrist. She is reading a script and throughout the play will not have the
faintest notion what is going on or where she is supposed to be. She stands
by the door nervously turning pages*

Pinch my bottom.
Mr Parrot What?
Fifi Pinch my bottom.

Parrot remains baffled

Top of page two.

Parrot finds the place, moves over to Fifi and pinches her bottom. Fifi stands up as if surprised. The vacuum cleaner noise stops

Mr Parrot Mon Dieu! I 'ave been assaulted.
Fifi That's my line. Mon Dieu! I 'ave been assaulted.

Parrot moves DL. *Fifi pulls him back*

Monsieur Parrot, it is you. What are you doing 'ere? You 'ave rented ze room next door.

As soon as Parrot starts to speak, he moves away again out of Fifi's reach

Mr Parrot The view is better in here, my little French pastry. One kiss, I implore you.
Fifi Non, monsieur! Take your 'ands off me! Let me go, let me go!

Parrot is nowhere near her. Fifi moves to him

Fifi (*sotto voce*) Kiss me.
Mr Parrot (*shaking his head*) No, I'm not doing that.

Fifi slaps him round the face. Parrot drops his script and fumbles for it

Fifi I will not let you take advantage of me. You are a married man.
Mr Parrot Where are we?
Fifi Page two.
Mr Parrot This must be our room, Frank.
Fifi Page *two*.
Mr Parrot I feel better now so let's sign the contracts.

Fifi finds the place for him

Fifi But my wife is a hundred miles away in London!
Mr Parrot But my husband ——
Fifi Wife!
Mr Parrot — is a hundred miles away in London.
Fifi Zat is what you sink, monsieur. Regardez-vous ze message on zat table.

As Parrot turns towards the telephone table, Fifi remembers with horror that there is no message there. Parrot searches on and under table for the message. His attention is attracted by:

Gordon peers from the wings

Gordon (*whispering*) Imagine it.

Parrot does so, putting the script under his arm, picking up an imaginary letter and studying it. Meanwhile Fifi, who has not seen this business, goes to the door C, and knocks on it surreptitiously

Fifi 'Oo is it? (*Ventriloquial; gruff*) Telegram! (*Normal*) Ah, bon. (*She opens the door and pretends to take delivery of a telegram*) Merci.

She hands the imaginary telegram to Parrot

'Ere is ze message, monsieur.
Mr Parrot (*referring to the imaginary letter*) What's this then?
Fifi What?
Mr Parrot This.
Fifi There's nothing there.

Parrot throws away the imaginary letter

(*Referring to an imaginary telegram*) Look at this.
Mr Parrot What?
Fifi This.
Mr Parrot There's nothing there either.
Fifi Imagine it.

Parrot does so

Gordon's hand waves a real piece of paper from the wings

Gordon Use this.
Mr Parrot (*referring to the imaginary telegram*) What's this then?
Gordon What?
Mr Parrot This.
Gordon There's nothing there. Read this,
Mr Parrot (*looking at the paper*) There's nothing on it.
Gordon Read the script!

Gordon exits

Mr Parrot (*reading the script*) "Reading message. My wife is coming here. What shall I do? I told her I was going to St Andrews for a golfing holiday whereas in reality I'm spending the weekend here with my mistress Brigitte. Knocking is heard off."

A knock at door D. Fifi pulls Parrot c

Gordon enters as George Barrett

Mr Barrett Good lord, if it isn't Roger Parrot. Fancy seeing you here.
Mr Parrot Why, it's George Barrett, isn't it? We haven't met since we were at Cambridge together.
Mr Barrett That's right. You were reading English.
Mr Parrot And you were reading palae ... palnt ... I can't read this.

He shows it to Fifi

Mr Barrett That's all behind me now. In recent years I've been in property. In fact I'm here in Paris with my secretary Mrs Carrott to complete a major business deal. What about you?
Mr Parrot Palaeontology.
Mr Barrett Yes.
Mr Parrot Is it me?
Fifi Yes.
Mr Barrett What about you?
Mr Parrot Oh, yes. Why, it's George Barrett, isn't it? We haven't met since we were at Cambridge together.
Mr Barrett That's right. You were reading English.
Mr Parrot And you were reading ... I've said this before, haven't I?
Fifi (*pointing at the script*) What about you ... monsieur?
Mr Parrot I'm spending a dirty weekend with my mistr ... pauses realizes he mustn't say mistress I mean my wife.
Mr Barrett A weekend with your wife! Then why were you making eyes at that gorgeous maid who was here a few moments ago?

Hearing this, Fifi frantically collects the vacuum cleaner and exits through door D

Mr Parrot You must be mistaken, George.
Mr Barrett Well anyway, why don't you pour us a couple of drinks, old man?

Mr Parrot What'll you have?
Mr Barrett Gin and tonic for me.

Fumbling with his script, Parrot knocks the gin bottle to the floor

Mr Barrett Make that a whisky and soda.

Parrot picks up the whisky bottle, takes off the top and drops the bottle

  On second thoughts I'll just have the soda.

Parrot places the glass on the wrong side of the syphon, presses plunger and squirts soda over his trousers. He hands Barrett the empty glass

Mr Parrot One gin and tonic.
Mr Barrett Cheers.
Mr Parrot Draining his glass. I wonder if you could do me a favour, George?
Mr Barrett Name it, old bean.
Mr Parrot Would you mind looking after my mistress I mean my wife this afternoon?
Mr Barrett Anything for an old ——
Mr Parrot No. Why?
Mr Barrett What?
Mr Parrot Why?
Mr Barrett Oh. Why?
Mr Parrot Because I'm expecting my wife ... I mean because there's something I must do in the Louvre.
Mr Barrett Anything for an old friend. Where is your good lady?
Mr Parrot Next door. I'll go and get her. Brigitte, darling, you look as ravishing as ever——
Mr Barrett No, Minnie. You go next door now.
Mr Parrot Sorry. Where?

Barrett points. Parrot walks L

Mr Barrett No, Minnie, that's a wall!

Parrot obligingly mimes stepping over a low wall

The Lights fade R. The Lights come up L

Mr Parrot Brigitte, how I look forward to these illicit weekends together.

He looks around for Brigitte Charot, who is not present. Then we hear an attempt being made to open door A. Nothing happens. Further attempts are made, which shake the set alarmingly

Mme Charot (*off*) What the bloody hell's the matter with this door? I can't get in. I can't get on the set. Someone has locked this door.
Mrs Reece (*off*) Thelma, be careful, for heaven's sake.
Mme Charot (*off*) What am I supposed to do? I can't get in.
Mrs Reece (*off*) Go round the other way.
Mme Charot (*off*) Get someone to do something about this.

Loud footsteps are heard followed by a crash outside door C

Mme Charot (*off*) Who left that bloody Hoover in the way?

> *Thelma, as the seductive Brigitte Charot, strides through door D and crosses R to L*

Mr Barrett You're walking through a wall, Thelma.
Mme Charot Shut up.

Mme Charot emerges into the lit area L

> Roger, ma chérie! 'Ow tall and masculine you look silhouetted against ze Arc de Triomphe.

She moves him into this position

> 'Ow I 'ave missed your passionate embrace and ze touch of your unshaven cheek. Come! To ze bed. We 'ave so much time to make up.

Parrot is pulled reluctantly towards the bed

Mr Parrot I'm not doing any kissing.
Mme Charot Kiss me, my English stallion.

Parrot distastefully kisses the air

> Oh! I am on fire! I burn! Take me!

She pulls Parrot on to the bed, which collapses beneath their weight

> I sink I felt ze earth move. Come, let me loosen your tie ... comme ça.

She struggles to loosen Parrot's tightly-knotted tie, pulling it over his head and removing first his spectacles and then his wig. Leaving him to replace these things, Mme Charot moves to the record-player, where she picks up two LPs

And now I will put on some sexy music. What do you prefer: 'Andel's 'Water Music' or Stevie Wonder?
Mr Parrot Handel's 'Water Music', please.
Mme Charot Moi aussi.

She takes the Handel record, puts it on the turntable and twiddles knobs but there is no sound

It begins very quietly.

The sound of the vacuum cleaner, then silence. Mme Charot removes the record from the record-player

Per'aps we will 'ave ze ozair side.

While the record is still in her hand, we hear the sound of Stevie Wonder. Mme Charot hurriedly replaces the record and returns to bed

Ah! Listen to 'ow 'Andel seems to suggest ze sun's rays twinkling on ze Thames.
Mr Parrot I have brought you a little token of my affection, my darling. It is there on the dressing-table.
Mme Charot Ah, 'ow extravagant you are, Roger. (*She gingerly picks up a half-full bottle of milk from the table*) Zis is ze most expensive perfume in ze 'ole of France.
Mr Parrot I know it is your favourite.
Mme Charot Ah, oui. "Forbidden Desire." (*She dabs behind her ears with distaste*) It unchains ze beast in me.
Mr Parrot Surrender to your animal instincts, my sex kitten. Oh, where'd you find that, Thelma? I left it by the tea urn and someone walked off with it ...

Offenbach's 'Apache Dance' is heard

Mme Charot Listen! Zat penniless musician in ze garret opposite is playing our song.
Mr Parrot Yes, I hear it. The dance of love. This isn't kissing again, is it?

They dance

Mme Charot (*panting*) You 'ave made a woman of me, Roger. Do you 'ave a cigarette, ma chèrie?

While Parrot is speaking, Mme Charot takes two cigarettes out of Parrot's top pocket and tries to stuff them into his mouth

Mr Parrot I have two, Brigitte, one for you and one for me. Yes, just like the old days. Do you remember how I would light them both, like I'm doing now, and then pass one to you ...? (*He spits out cigarettes*) You know I don't smoke.

Mme Charot retrieves the broken cigarette and pretends to draw on it

Mme Charot You were zere. So was I. Maybe millions of people passed by.

Mr Parrot And when I looked into your eyes all I could think of was ... (*she turns the page*) ... my English bulldog.

Mme Charot What?

Mr Parrot That's what it says.

Mme Charot You've turned over two pages.

Mr Parrot Sorry. All I could think of was moonlight in the Tropics.

Mme Charot You say ze sweetest things.

Mr Parrot There's something I have to ask you, Brigitte.

Mme Charot I am yours to command, mon amour.

Mr Parrot I've never told you this before, but I ... what's this? It's smudged with mascara.

Mme Charot You work for the Secret Service.

Mr Parrot I work for the Secret Service.

Mme Charot Ah! quelle surprise.

Mr Parrot And for reasons of international security you must pretend to the man next door that you're my wife.

Mme Charot What will 'appen if I refuse?

Mr Parrot You'll bring about the collapse of Western civilization.

Mme Charot What nonsense! I refuse.

Mr Parrot Do not refuse!

Mme Charot I refuse! Let everysing collapse.

Door A promptly falls off its hinges. Mme Charot screams and jumps up

Mr Parrot Do it for me, my love.

Mme Charot I will do it only for you.

Mr Parrot Come with me.

He takes Mme Charot's hand and begins to lead her across the stage to other room. Mme Charot jerks him back and leads him out of door A

The Lights come up to full

Mme Charot enters through door D expecting Parrot to follow her in. He doesn't. Mme Charot looks out of the door then exits again

Parrot emerges through door A, looks around and goes out

Mme Charot enters through door D, registers to Barrett that she can't find Parrot, and exits through door C

Parrot at once enters through door A and turns to leave again

Mr Parrot Thelma!

Hearing this, Barrett is just in time to see Parrot disappearing. He runs after him

Mr Barrett Minnie!

He exits through door A

Mme Charot enters through door C to find Barrett gone. She slams her way out again

Felicity, dressed as a Chorus Girl, pops through door A then disappears

Mrs Reece, dressed in a pantomime animal skin, enters through door C, then thinks better of it and exits again

Parrot finally comes through the correct door (D). Barrett and Mme Charot enter through door A and see him

Mr Parrot Ah, there you are, George. I'd like to introduce you to my wife.

Barrett and Mme Charot walk R and then shake hands with each other

Mr Barrett How do you do, Mrs Parrot.
Mme Charot Enchantée...
Mr Parrot (*prompting*) And please call me Brigitte ...
Mme Charot (*to Parrot*) That's a pause! (*To Barrett*) And please call me Brigitte. (*To Parrot*) Where are you going, darling?

She propels Parrot to door D

Mr Parrot I've got to meet my wife at four o'clock I mean I'm going to the Louvre. He exits.

He doesn't. Instead, noticing a dangling hem on Mme Charot's dress, he takes a needle from his lapel and kneels to do some tacking

Mme Charot And meanwhile I will become acquainted wiz your attractive friend, Monsieur Barrett.

Mr Barrett You flatter me, Brigitte.

Mme Charot Non, non, non, it is true. Your body is a shrine to your public school physical education.

Mr Barrett I try and keep myself in shape.

Parrot has crawled round Mme Charot so that she is now kneeling between her and Barrett. Having finished sewing, Parrot stands up. Thinking she is Barrett, Mme Charot grasps him in an embrace

Mme Charot You are an Adonis and I am your slave. I tremble wiz desire for you, my English bulldog.

Barrett tries to embrace Mme Charot. Parrot is now sandwiched in between Mme Charot and Barrett. Mme Charot runs her fingers through Barrett's hair

Mr Barrett But you are a married woman.

Mme Charot moves her hand from Barrett's head to Parrot's head. She wonders why she is embracing two people

Mme Charot My 'usband will never find out ... (*She turns to see Parrot*) Minnie, go *away.*

Mr Parrot Oh, am I off?

Mr Parrot wanders out of door D

Mme Charot Prepare me a dry Tia Maria, my darling, while I go to ze bathroom to slip into somesing more comfortable.

She is confronted with the upside-down door (B), which she is unable to climb over

But why go to ze bathroom when ze kitchen is 'ere?

She opens door C and is greeted with the sight of Minnie reading her script She slams the door and moves to door D

Where does this lead?
Mr Barrett The hotel foyer.
Mme Charot I will change in zere.

She attempts to open door D, but the handle has been put on hinged side. She eventually realizes this and pushes the opposite side of the door to exit

Mr Barrett By Jove! Parrot's wife is a sex maniac. She's going to wreck my major business deal. If only my wife were here. Then perhaps Mrs Parrot would leave me alone.

A knock at door D

Come in.

Fifi enters

Fifi Madame Carrott ... aaggghhh!

She is catapulted back into the wings as though her apron string has been caught on a nail. After a moment she enters with less confidence. Then she realizes she has forgotten her next line. She returns to the wings

(*Off*) Prompt.
Minnie (*off*) [*Inaudible line*].

Fifi returns to Barrett, but doesn't have the courage to repeat what she heard. She returns to the wings

Fifi (*off*) Sorry?
Minnie (*off*) [*Inaudible line*].

Pause

Fifi returns to Barrett

Fifi (*finally to Barrett*) [*Inaudible line*].
Mr Barrett What?

Fifi returns to the wings

Fifi (*off*)I can't hear you.
Minnie (*off*) Your secretary Madame Carrott is here.

Fifi returns to Barrett

Fifi Your secretary Madame Carrott is here.
Mr Barrett Perfect. Show her in.

Mrs Reece, playing the soberly-dressed Mary Carrott, enters with a briefcase. Minnie, still reading her script, wanders in behind her

Fifi turns her round and pushes her out in front of her

Mrs Carrott Good-afternoon, Mr Barrett. I've brought the contracts for you and Monsieur Charot to sign.
Mr Barrett Never mind about that now. There's something you've got to do for me. You've got to pretend to be my wife.
Mrs Carrott Whatever for?
Mr Barrett I can't explain now. Just do as I say.

Mme Charot bursts in through door D wearing a baby-doll nightie

Mme Charot Embrassé-moi, mon imbécile!

Black-out

Mrs Carrott No, too early, Malcolm. We haven't quite finished, dear. What are you two playing at up there?

The Lights come up to full

Thank you. (*To Mme Charot*) Come in again, dear.
Mme Charot Tch.

She listlessly exits and enters

Mrs Carrott (*to the lighting box*) And you behave yourselves.
Mme Charot Embrassé-moi ...

Fifi enters through door A. Minnie stumbles in behind her; she is now dressed as flamboyant French businessman Jacques Charot

Fifi Voilà, monsieur! Ze manager say zis room is vacant. I sink he is wrong, but I am only ze maid ...

Mrs Carrott Felicity! Felicity! Woo-oo! Have to stop you there, dear, or we'll get confused. We're still acting over here, you see. But it's not your fault, it's Malcolm's. I don't think he's got his mind on the job.
Mme Charot Malcolm?

Fifi grabs M Charot, who is already wandering aimlessly round the set, and they exit through door A

Mrs Carrott Carry on, Thelma.
Mme Charot I'm not going out again.
Mrs Carrott All right.
Mme Charot (*with no expression*) Embrassé-moi, mon imbécile.
Mr Barrett Ah, Brigitte: may I introduce you to my wife?
Mme Charot (*with no expression*) Oh, no. You have deceived me, you beast.

She exits through door D

Mrs Carrott And freeze.

She and Barrett freeze, but the Lights stay

Malcolm!

Fifi enters through door A, leading M. Charot, whom she manoeuvres from one part of the room to another

Fifi Voilà, monsieur! Ze manager say zis room is vacant. I sink he is wrong, but I am only ze maid...
Mrs Carrott Malcolm! Black-out over here, please!

Fifi guides M. Charot to the window

Fifi You will note ze charming view of ze Arc de Triomphe ——
Mrs Carrott Joyce! Will you put him down? We need a black-out!
Fifi And over 'ere ...

Black-out followed by screams and thuds. The Lights come up L revealing that Fifi and M. Charot have fallen over the bed

M. Charot Oh, Felicity, that must have been my full weight ...
Fifi Yes, it *was* your full weight ...
M. Charot And on your poorly leg as well.

Fifi has scrambled to her feet

Fifi Over 'ere is your posture-sprung bed.
M. Charot Are we acting again? All right. I can smell perfume. My wife
    Brigitte's perfume.
Fifi A coincidence, monsieur.

Fifi seats Charot on a chair

M. Charot Very well. He sits down. Kindly tell me when Mr Barrett and his
    secretary Mrs Carrott have arrived. We have some important documents
    to sign.
Fifi Zey are 'ere already, monsieur. I will inform zem of your presence.

She goes to exit through door A. Charot gets up and follows her

    No, freeze! You freeze!

*As the Lights L fade, Charot can be seen shivering with cold. The Lights come
up R revealing Barrett and Mrs Carrott waiting for a cue*

M. Charot 'Scuse me.

Mrs Carrott turns to her

    Can't see to read.
Mrs Carrott Ssshh.

*The vacuum cleaner noise is heard momentarily. Nothing else happens.
Barrett and Mrs Carrott look uneasily at each other. Finally there is a crash
off stage followed shortly afterwards by a knock at door D*

    (*With relief*) Oh, there's someone at the door.

*She crosses to the door, opens it and is greeted with the sight of Fifi pulling
up her skirt with one hand and trying to fix her cap with the other*

Fifi (*panting*) Sorry ... forgot ... then I fell over the Hoover ... sorry ...
    Monsieur Charot is 'ere to see Mr Barrett and you, Mrs Carrott.
Mrs Carrott I'm not Mrs Carrott, I'm Mrs Barrett.
Mr Barrett No she's not. She's Mrs Carrott. (*To Mrs Carrott*) You're only
    Mrs Barrett to Mrs Parrot. Got it?
Mrs Carrott I'm only Mrs Barrett to Mrs Parrot. Got it.

Fifi disappears, removing her skirt

Mr Barrett (*to Fifi*) Tell Monsieur Charot ... (*He realizes Fifi is gone. Calling after her*) Tell Monsieur Charot that Mr Barrett and Mrs Carrott will join him directly.

Fifi pops back into view, holding her costume together. She looks confused and dashes away again

(*To Mrs Carrott*) Now I'll stay and deal with Mrs Parrot ...
Mrs Carrott Right.

She hurries out door D

Mr Barrett And you go next door and stall Monsieur Charot. (*He goes to door B*) All right, Mrs Parrot: come out of this bathroom.

The Lights R fade

Barrett exits

The Lights come up L revealing M. Charot sitting studying a knitting pattern and winding wool on to a ball from a skein

There is a knock at door A, which is ignored. Another, also ignored

Mrs Carrott appears in the door frame. She carries the briefcase

Important: M. Charot does not move from the chair throughout the scene

Mrs Carrott Monsieur Charot?

No reply

Minnie! You can't do that now.
M. Charot I told you, Mrs Reece, I promised to have this matinée jacket finished by tomorrow evening. You know, my niece...
Mrs Carrott But we're acting. Put it away. It's your turn.
M. Charot Er — where are we? Mrs Carrott knocks on door. Right. Hearing knock on door. Who is it?
Mrs Carrott Good question. Er — Mary Carrott, Monsieur Charot. I'm only Mrs Barrett to Mrs Parrot.

M. Charot One moment, Madame Carrott, while I finish shaving. Violà. Now I will slip into this dressing-gown and I will be presentable. Bonjour, Madame. Please forgive me for keeping such a beautiful woman waiting.
Mrs Carrott Oh! a kiss on the hand. How Continental.

She moves swiftly to Charot and sticks her hand under his nose, but he pushes it away in order to read his script

M. Charot A tribute to your charm and elegance, Madame.
Mrs Carrott You are too kind. Here are the contracts.

She reaches into the briefcase and realizes it is empty. Flustering slightly, she exits through door A

Charot carries on regardless

M. Charot A formidable wad of papers to be sure. And yet they seem perfectly in order. But wait! I notice that Clause 5 of Sub-Section B of the Second Schedule states that the executor of the one part and the lessee of the second part shall execute contemporaneously herewith all other sums payable thereunder but not heretofore. I feel this contradicts Clause 3f of Sub-Section A ...

He breaks off as he glances up to discover that Mrs Carrott has gone. He thinks a moment then absent-mindedly continues his woolwinding

Mrs Carrott appears in doorway A

Mrs Carrott Can't find them.

A sheaf of papers is thrown over the top of the flats on to the stage

Oh. Air mail.

She picks up the blank sheets and puts them on Charot's lap. Charot places the skein on her outstretched hands and continues winding

Your signature is required here, here and here.
M. Charot Where is Monsieur Barrett?
Mrs Carrott He will join us in two minutes.
M. Charot You mean we have two minutes alone together?
Mrs Carrott Why, yes.
M. Charot Then let me press my body next to yours, dear Madame Carrott. I am crazy about your long English legs.

Mrs Carrott Please, Monsieur, I beg of you: do not come any closer.
M. Charot Grant me one glimpse of your dimpled knees I beseech you. He throws her on the bed.
Mrs Carrott Stop this at once, Monsieur Charot. Remove your hands from my thighs. Oh! oh! oh!

Barrett appears in doorway A, trips and falls on to the stage

M. Charot Did I hear somebody knock?
Mr Barrett (*knocking on the floor*) May I come in?
Mrs Carrott Mr Barrett!
Mr Barrett Mrs Carrott! What are you doing in bed with Monsieur Char ... (*he realizes*) ... what are you doing in bed on your own?

M. Charot resumes reading the knitting pattern

.

Mrs Carrott I can explain everything. (*Aside*) How can I dampen Monsieur Charot's ardour without jeapardizing Mr Barrett's business deal? I know. I'll pretend Mr Barrett's my husband. (*To Charot*) Monsieur Charot: this is my husband.
Mr Barrett What?
Mrs Carrott (*to Barrett*) Say you're my husband.
M. Charot (*looking up uncertainly*) What?

Mrs Carrott motions M. Charot to read his script

Mrs Carrott Monsieur Charot: this is my husband.
M. Charot (*prompting Barrett*) What.
Mrs Carrott This is my husband.
Mr Barrett What?
Mrs Carrott (*to Barrett*) Say you're my husband.
M. Charot What?
Mr Barrett (*to Charot*) What?
Mrs Carrott Say you're my husband.
M. Charot This is my husband.
Mrs Carrott (*to Charot*) What?
M. Charot Say you're my husband.
Mrs Carrott No, this ... (*indicating Barrett*) ... is my husband.
Mr Barrett What?
Mrs Carrott Say you're my husband.
Mr Barrett (*prompting Charot*) What.
Mrs Carrott No, you say "I am her husband".
M. Charot I am her husband.

Mrs Carrott No, he ... (*indicating Barrett*) ... says "I am her husband."

Mr Barrett I am her husband.

M. Charot What?

Mrs Carrott This is my husband.

Pause

M. Charot What?

Mrs Carrott (*shaking her head*) This is my husband.

Mr Barrett What?

Mrs Carrott Say you're my husband.

Mr Barrett I am her husband.

Mrs Carrott (*prompting Charot*) What!

M. Charot What?

Mrs Carrott This is my husband.

Long pause

Mr Barrett (*shrugging*) What?

Mrs Carrott No, no, no.

She moves L behind Barrett to Charot, taking the wool with her and entangling Barrett. She then leans over Charot's script and runs through the dialogue, pointing at the appropriate speakers

This is my husband ... What?... Say you're my husband ... What?... I am her husband ... What?... This is my husband ... (*pointing at Charot*) ... So this is your husband?

M. Charot Oh, it's me.

Mrs Carrott Yes.

M. Charot Sorry.

Mrs Carrott returns R, crossing in front of Barrett and further entangling him. Pause

(*Hopefully*) What?

Mrs Carrott No. The line underneath that.

M. Charot Oh. He gets off the bed and faces Barrett.

Mrs Carrott crosses again to M. Charot

Mrs Carrott That's a stage direction, Minnie. I keep telling you: don't read the things in brackets.

M. Charot Sorry. Er — so this is your husband?

Mrs Carrott Keep going. (*She returns*)

M. Charot Do not be alarmed, Monsieur Carrott. Your wife contracted a sudden leg cramp and I was massaging it.

Mrs Carrott I feel better now so let's sign the contracts.

She moves L behind Barrett to Charot, causing further entanglement. During ensuing dialogue Mrs Carrott and Barrett try to extricate themselves to no avail

M. Charot I cannot sign the contracts without Monsieur Barrett.

Mr Barrett But I'm here.

Mrs Carrott No, you're not.

Mr Barrett Aren't I?

Mrs Carrott Of course you're not, darling. You're Mr Carrott, aren't you?

Mr Barrett Of course I am. How silly of me to forget.

M. Charot Where is Monsieur Barrett?

Mrs Carrott ⎤ (*together*) ⎰ He's downstairs.
Mr Barrett ⎦   ⎱ He's next door.

Mrs Carrott He's downstairs ... next door ... in the bistro. Shall we go and join him?

M. Charot That is an excellent idea.

Barrett and Mrs Carrott stand waiting for Charot to get up, but he doesn't and Mrs Carrott has to help him out of the chair and push him out of door A

Charot exits

Mr Barrett What on earth's going on, Mrs Carrott?

Mrs Carrott Monsieur Charot tried to seduce me.

Mr Barrett So that's why you were in bed ... on your own.

Mrs Carrott Yes. And to prevent an argument, I had to pretend you were Mr Carrott. There was nothing else I could do. My ... hands were tied.

Mr Barrett I can see that now.

Mrs Carrott But what shall we do when we get to the bistro and Mr Barrett isn't there?

Mr Barrett That's all right. My friend Roger Parrot owes me a favour. I'll get him to pretend he's me.

Wrapped in wool, they shuffle out of door A

The Lights fade L. The Lights come up R

Felicity, as Mrs Constance Barrett, enters through door D

Mrs Barrett George? George, it's four o'clock. Where are you? It's Constance here — your wife. Strange! I wonder where he could be?

A thud against door D

Perhaps this is him now. (*She opens the door*)

Minnie — dressed half as M. Charot and half as Mr Parrott — tumbles in, juggling with the script and wrapped in wool

Mr Parrot I'm ... (*He turns over several pages of script*)
Mrs Barrett (*prompting him*) Roger Parrot.
Mr Parrot Roger Parrot.
Mrs Barrett Why, I'd never have guessed. You must be my husband George's old chum from Cambridge. (*Prompting him*) Yes, I am.
Mr Parrot Yes, I am.

She holds out her hand, but retrieves it when Parrot doesn't take it. Just as she does this, Parrot puts out his hand, then retrieves it. Mrs Barrett puts out her hand, but just misses him. Continue ad nauseam

Mrs Barrett George has told me so much about you.

Pause

Who am I? I'm Constance Barrett. I telephoned earlier and left a message with Fifi the French maid that I'd be arriving at four o'clock.

Pause

Yes, I did. Page twenty-three. By the expression on your face I guess that Fifi muddled up our very similar names and told you that *your* wife was arriving at four. Am I right?
Mr Parrot (*boldly guessing*) No!
Mrs Barrett Yes.
Mr Parrot Yes.
Mrs Barrett Well, I wonder where my husband is?
Mr Parrot I don't even know where I am.

Mrs Barrett moves to door C

Mrs Barrett Perhaps he's in the kitchen. (*She opens the door and is surprised to find nobody there. Wool is stretched across the door frame*) Ah! There's a half-naked woman in here. Who are you?

A pause. Mme Charot makes a couple of attempts to enter, but something is restraining her. Finally she catapults through the door C, entangled in wool. Simultaneously Mr Parrot is jerked out of door D and in through door C behind Mme Charot

Mme Charot I am Madame Parrot.
Mrs Barrett Roger's wife?
Mme Charot Oui.
Mr Parrot No.
Mrs Barrett Yes or no?
Mme Charot } (*together*) { Oui.
Mr Parrot } { No.
Mrs Barrett What are you doing in George's kitchen?
Mme Charot What is it to you?
Mrs Barrett I happen to be his wife.
Mme Charot Do not be ridiculous. I 'ave already met his wife.
Mrs Barrett What!?
Mme Charot Mais oui. And from ze bathroom window I 'ave seen 'im escorting 'er to ze bistro across ze road.
Mr Parrot Next door.
Mme Charot Look! You read your lines, I'll read mine.
Mrs Barrett My husband a bigamist! Oh!

About to cry, she reaches for a handkerchief in her handbag, but when she unclips the bag, it falls apart, depositing its contents on the floor. Parrot takes Mme Charot aside

Mr Parrot Don't worry, Mrs Barrett. I'm sure your husband will explain why he got married again without telling you.

Mme Charot irritably pushes Parrot back to Mrs Barrett

Mme Charot Not me — her!
Mr Parrot (*to Mrs Barrett*) You wanton hussy! Get out of that saucy négligé immediately.
Mme Charot Anything you say, Roger.

She moves to take off the nightie. Black-out

Everyone exits

The Lights come up L

*Mrs Reece, as Mr Frank Carrott, and Gordon, as Mrs Virginia Parrot,
enter through door A. Mr Carrott carries suitcases*

Mrs Parrot This must be our room, Frank. Come in quickly and close the
door.

Carrott realizes this is not possible. He puts down the cases

Mr Carrott Together at last, Virginia. I can't tell you how much I've been
looking forward to this weekend.
Mrs Parrot Are you sure nothing can go wrong?
Mr Carrott Positive.

*Hopelessly entwined together, Parrot, Mme Charot and Mrs Barrett bounce
behind door A,* R *to* L

My wife Mary is on a business trip with her employer George Barrett, the
well-known property tycoon, and your husband Roger is on a golfing
holiday in St Andrews.
Mrs Parrot Then take me in a lingering embrace.

They sit on the bed. Carrott takes Mrs Parrot in a lingering embrace

*After a few moments Parrot can be seen making attempts to get through
door A, but he keeps being hauled out of sight*

Mr Parrot Come in here, Brigitte ...

*We hear this line twice more before Parrot finally manages to get on to the
stage accompanied by Mme Charot and, behind her, Mrs Barrett. They are
all tied together. Mrs Barrett, who is not supposed to be making an
entrance, is pulling in the opposite direction*

Come in here, Brigitte. We can have some privacy.
Mrs Parrot Ah! my husband!
Mr Parrot My wife!

*Mr Carrott jumps off bed and with great difficulty manages to drop his
trousers revealing Union Jack shorts. The window flat collapses on to the
stage. Screaming, Parrot, Mme Charot and Mrs Barrett leap out of the way*

Black-out. The sound of the vacuum cleaner then music: Orpheus in the Underworld. *The House Lights come up. Door A is replaced, the bed is repaired. A small table is set* C, *with a mixing bowl, cake ingredients and cooking utensils on it*

ENTR'ACTE

Spot on Mrs Reece as she mounts the stage

Mrs Reece Hallo, ladies and gentlemen. Are you all having a nice time? Everybody enjoying themselves? What about the Frenchies? 'Allo! Comment ça va? Dites-moi: préférez-vous les Farndale Ladies ou la Royal Shakespeare Company? Oh, you're just saying that! Well, we're going to have a lot more fun in a minute because in part two things begin to go wrong! But just before we start, I've got one or two announcements to make: first of all there was a misprint in last week's Guild Newsletter. I don't know if any of you have your copies, do you? If you do and you turn to page eight you'll see that Mrs Ladbrook is advertising for a companion to help her deal with her enormous male. Well, at the risk of disappointing prospective applicants, I really must point out that "mail" should have been spelled m-a-i-l.

Mrs Reece dons a fashionable apron and moves to the cookery table

And now a special treat, a preview of the dish Mrs Dabney will be preparing at next Thursday evening's cookery class. It's something that will appeal to your dinner guests from far and wide, a Black Forest zabaglione sponge in ouzo with a sauerkraut topping. First of all you'll need to separate the yolks from six eggs. And the key word here is "delicacy".

She attempts to crack a (fake) egg on the side of her mixing bowl, which breaks in two

Well, let's assume the yolks are now separated. Next we're going to blend them with three ounces of finely-sifted flour...

She picks up bag of flour; bottom falls out and leaves flour on table

And this mixing can be done in a Moulinex or with a hand whisk.

The whisk's handle comes off in her hand

Although preferably not this one. Basically you throw in any other foreign things you may have lying around but don't forget to add a pair of

Österreichische Schlosserbuben, which are just as tasty the following day with chips. Divide into two seven-inch cake tins and bake for twenty-five minutes at gas mark three. Well, to save time I've got a cake we prepared earlier — and here it is.

Thelma enters carrying a plate containing a tinfoil-covered cake

I don't know about you, but my mouth's watering already! May we have the grand unveiling, Thelma?

Thelma uncovers squashed sponge with indented footprint

Mrs Reece Well, it's not exactly in pristine condition, I'm afraid.
Thelma Felicity trod in it.
Mrs Reece It is so dark back there, isn't it? Well, if you can imagine it without the footprint, I think you'll agree that it's ... jolly nice. Now I wonder if anyone here tonight is going to be able to guess the weight of that little lot?

She gestures towards Thelma, who bristles

I'm talking about the cake. Any guesses, ladies and gentlemen? We do have a prize for the correct answer so just call out and you may be the lucky one.

She rejects several guesses from the audience because the cake is lighter than they imagine. Finally she picks on a man who has guessed the "correct" weight

Absolutely spot on. Who said that? Was it a gentleman? Yes. Would you like to come up and join us?

While the member of the audience is making his way to the stage, Thelma exits with the cake. Minnie enters and removes the cookery table

Mrs Reece asks the audience member's name

There's something I'd like you to do for me, if you wouldn't mind? You probably didn't notice, but we've been having a bit of trouble with the scenery. Our producer's been trying to get it up in the interval, but it's not one of his good nights. I wonder if you'd be so good as to put your shoulder under it?

Mrs Reece ad libs with the audience member while he raises the window flat

That's it. Now just hold it in position while the girls have a fiddle with it round the back. Can we let it go now? Good. Let's move out of harm's way, just in case. Tell me, do you do any weight-training? Oh, what a pity. Because we have to get this piano up to the second floor. Never mind. You've been very helpful so we've got this little present for you. It's [*well-known cookery book*]. And if you take this home, maybe a little later in the week, either your wife or your girlfriend will surprise you with a bun in the oven.

The audience member returns to his seat

And now it's time for more adventures in our crazy apartment house in Paris ...

Thelma enters, wrapped in a tricolour

Thelma, what are you doing?
Thelma My song.
Mrs Reece But it's been cut, dear.
Thelma By whom?
Mrs Reece I had to take the initiative. We're running late and time and tide wait for no woman.
Thelma I will not allow my artistry to be compromised so that you can watch [*television programme*].
Mrs Reece That has nothing to do with it.

She eases Thelma towards door A

I'll tell you what. We'll slip you in somewhere else. What about tomorrow morning when we're clearing up?
Thelma But there'll be nobody here to watch me.
Mrs Reece That's not true, Thelma. I know for a fact that the caretaker will be here with his wife, Doreen, and then the vicar always pops in to dust the flower display in the vestibule ... (*to the lighting box*) Action ...! and Mrs Wolstenholme will definitely be coming in to collect her tablecloth ...

They exit

The House Lights go down

BLACK-OUT

ACT II

Full stage Lights up. Immediately we hear the sound of the Hoover

Fifi rushes on through door D with the Hoover, plugs it in and begins cleaning. The telephone rings. She stops cleaning; the sound effect stops. She goes to the telephone and picks up the receiver

Fifi 'Allo! Ici les Chambres du Oo-la-la, an apartment 'ouse in ze Champs-Elysées populair wiz Englishmen spending business weekends in Paris. Je suis Fifi ze maid. 'Oo is zat? Mais oui, Madame Barrett, I will give your 'usband a message avec plaisir...

Mrs Reece appears at door A

Mrs Reece Felicity! Felicity!

Fifi looks round

Wrong act.

Mrs Reece withdraws

Fifi pulls herself together and starts again

Fifi 'Allo! Ici les Chambres du Oo-la-la. Je suis Fifi ze maid. 'oo is zat? Ah, non, Monsieur, je regrette. We 'ave no vacancies at ze moment. In fact we are so overcrowded zat four people 'ave been accidentally booked into ze same room. Oui, quelle dommage. Au revoir.

She hangs up. The sound of the Hoover is heard. A knock at door D

(*Shouting*) Ah! 'oo can zat be? (*She opens the door*)

Thelma—as Jack Garrett, a plumber in overalls, carrying a toolbag— is standing there fuming

Mr Garrett Joyce!

The sound effect cuts off

Mrs Reece appears behind Mr Garrett

Mrs Reece You have no idea how stiff that knob is getting up there.
Mr Garrett Oil it then!
Mrs Reece I did try in the interval, dear. But I couldn't get in. They'd locked the door. Come along now, on with the motley!

She disappears, closing the door

Mr Garrett My mistress.
Fifi My lover.

Keeping one eye on the lighting box, Garrett kisses his way up Fifi's arm

Mr Garrett I had to see you, my little pot of French mustard. I was unblocking a toilet and I could think only of you.
Fifi Non, non, Jack! We cannot keep meeting like zis. I 'ave a wife and you 'ave an 'usband.
Mr Garrett But I am a man and you are a woman.
Fifi You always know 'ow to persuade me. Quick — we can share ten precious minutes in ze bathroom.

She pulls him towards door B, then thinks better of it

Zere is a quick way to ze bathroom through ze kitchen.

They exit through door C. Simultaneously Barrett and Parrot enter through door D

Mr Barrett Now look here, old man, correct me if I'm wrong, but you seem to have two wives here.
Mr Parrot So do you.
Mr Barrett Ah, yes, but I can explain that.
Mr Parrot Go on then.
Mr Barrett Well, it's really quite simple.

He sits L. During the ensuing dialogue Parrot blows his nose, inadvertently removing his moustache into his handkerchief. Later Barrett notices Parrot's naked upper lip and tries to draw Parrot's attention to it. Parrot takes a while to catch on. He then feels around his face, and checks his clothes and the floor, in an effort to find the moustache. Failing in this, he discovers an eyebrow pencil in his pocket and raises his script in front of his face in order not to be seen pencilling in a new moustache. When he self-consciously lowers the script, we see the scrawled and lopsided results

Mrs Barrett is my wife, and my secretary, Mrs Carrott, is my ex-wife.

Mr Parrot That's a coincidence because Brigitte, the ex-wife of your business partner, Monsieur Charot, is my wife, and Mrs Parrot, who's now having an affair with your ex-wife's husband, is my ex-wife.

Mr Barrett Now I understand. Roger, could you do me a favour, old sport?

Mr Parrot Delighted, old bean.

Mr Barrett Could you tell your wife's ex-husband that I'm my ex-wife's husband?

Mr Parrot But if you're your ex-wife's husband, who's your wife's husband?

Mr Barrett You. If he thinks you're me, he'll sign the contracts.

Mr Parrot But if I'm your wife's husband, and you're your ex-wife's husband, who's your ex-wife's husband?

Mr Barrett He doesn't matter. He's having an affair with your ex-wife.

Mr Parrot Of course. Well, I'll do it on one condition.

Mr Barrett Name it, old fruit.

Mr Parrot My wife's ex-husband, your ex-wife and her lover who is, of course, you, have been accidentally booked into the room I booked for my wife and me. So you let my wife and me come in here.

Mr Barrett Well, let's get this straight: you'll be me and I'll be my ex-wife's husband if I let myself use my own room.

Mr Parrot Precisely.

Mr Barrett Done. I'll go and get your wife's ex-husband and bring him up here.

A knock on door D

Come in. (*He pushes the door sharply*)

A cry from behind it, then Mme Charot enters, holding her nose

Ah, Mrs Parrot: I'm just going to fetch Monsieur Charot.

Mme Charot Ah! My 'usband is 'ere?

Mr Barrett Yes, he's over here.

Mme Charot screams then realizes that Barrett is referring to Parrot

Barrett exits through door D

Mme Charot rushes to Parrot

Mme Charot Quick! My 'usband, Monsieur Charot, is coming. We must 'ide. But, where, where?

Mr Parrot The bathroom.

Mme Charot waits in vain for Parrot to open door B. She does so herself. Fifi screams off. Mme Charot closes the door

No, the kitchen. Follow me.

Mme Charot grabs Parrot and drags him through door C. Simultaneously, Carrott enters door D

Mr Carrott At last! An empty room where I can be alone with my mistress, Mrs — er — Thingumyjig — Parrot. There's just time to wash my hands before she arrives.

He opens door B. Mr Garrett screams off. Carrott slams the door

Good heavens! Fifi the maid is having a bath with the plumber. I shall have to wash my hands in the kitchen.

He opens door C. Mme Charot screams off. Carrott slams the door

Great Scott! My mistress's husband in the arms of my mistress's employer's business partner's wife.

Mrs Parrot enters through door D

Mrs Parrot Is this the empty room you meant, darling?
Mr Carrott No, darling. It's occupied. By your husband.
Mrs Parrot My husband?
Mr Carrott Yes, he's making love to the plumber.
Mrs Parrot What?
Mr Carrott I mean he's making love to the other part Thelma's playing. Quickly, we must hide.
Mrs Parrot Where?
Mr Carrott Under this occasional table.

They both attempt to crawl under the small table DC and are completely visible

Parrot is pushed through door C

Mr Parrot I thought I saw my wife's lover. He exits without noticing the lovers hidden under the table.

Parrot is pulled out. Simultaneously Felicity, playing Fifi's husband Jojo in striped sweater with onions round the neck, enters door D

Jojo Fifi! Zis is your 'usband Jojo. I know you are in 'ere wiz your lover so come out immediatement. (*He begins opening doors and looking round them*)

Taking the table with them, Carrott and Mrs Parrot begin to crawl out R

Do not try any of your tricks, ma chèrie. I warn you I 'ave eyes in ze back of my 'ead.

Mr Carrott Sorry, dear, which is the way out?

Jojo Here.

He leads them to door D and opens it

Mr Carrott All right, dear. we'll manage. Carry on speaking.

He and Mrs Parrot struggle in the doorway

Jojo Ah, quelle catastrophe! My English mistress Mary Carrott is coming down ze corridor.

Mr Carrott Don't be silly. That's me. I'm not ready.

Jojo I haven't got any more lines.

Mr Carrott Make something up.

He and Mrs Parrot exit with the table

Jojo is left standing like a lemon

Jojo (*out of character*) Yes, here she comes now. Down the corridor. Getting closer and closer to this room. Oh dear, she's fallen over. She's fallen over and hurt her leg. Now she's being rushed to hospital. Oh dear, now she's in traction. And now she's having a heart transplant. This could take some time.

Mrs Reece puts her head round door D

Mrs Reece Who did you say was coming — Mr Carrott or Mrs Carrott?

Jojo Mrs Carrott.

Mrs Reece Oh, lord.

She pops out of sight and slams the door

Jojo I can't think of anything else to say.

Thelma strides in through door D, wrapped in tricolour and carrying two saucepan lids

Thelma Don't worry, Felicity. I shall now sing a song that was cut earlier by Madame Chairman.

Mrs Reece (*off*) Thelma, I said you could do it tomorrow morning...

Thelma I have a prior engagement tomorrow morning. I'm collecting my award for Twin-Set Wearer of the Year.

She hands saucepan lids to Jojo

Keep time and don't upstage me.

(*Singing*)   Allons enfants de la Patrie,
                 Le jour de gloire est arrivé.
                 And I'm watching you like a hawk, Joyce:
                 Kindly keep your hands to yourself!
                 L'étendard sanglant est levé.
                 Entendez-vous dans les campagnes —
                 Malcolm! I'm talking to you:
                 I'm wise to all your little tricks.
                 You wait until I get you home!

Gordon, with a washboard, and Minnie, with spoons, enter through door D and play along

                 Aux armes, citoyens!
                 Formez vos bataillons,
                 Marchons, marchons!
                 Don't push your luck!
                 The worst is yet to come!
                 (*To the others*) That's called showbiz, kids.

All exit except Jojo. Mrs Reece looks in door D

Mrs Reece All right, I'm ready. And I'm Mrs Carrott, right?

Jojo Yes. Ah, my mistress is ready. Oh ... I can't remember where we are.

Mrs Reece You're hiding.

Jojo I'm hiding in the bathroom.

Thelma (*off*) No!

Jojo Why not?

Thelma (*off*) Because I'm in here with your wife.

Jojo Sorry. I will 'ide in ze foyer. (*He moves to door D*)

Mrs Carrott, Barrett and Mme Charot enter

I'm not here. I'm hiding.

Mrs Carrott Where?
Jojo I can't remember.
Mrs Carrott Bathroom.
Mme Charot I'm in there with his wife.
Mrs Carrott Who's in the kitchen?
Mme Charot I am.
Mrs Carrott With whom?
Mme Charot Mr Parrot.
Mrs Carrott Oh, he doesn't matter. (*To Jojo*) Kitchen.

Jojo is exiting through door C when Mrs Carrott picks up a chair and hands it to him

Oh, and take this chair with you. It's getting awfully cramped out here.

Jojo exits

Well now, at last we can sign the contra —— (*She thinks*) Mr Parrot's supposed to be out here.
Mme Charot No, he's not.
Mrs Carrott Yes, he is. It's the contract scene. And you're not supposed to be here.
Mme Charot Yes, I am.
Mrs Carrott No, you're not. You're the plumber in the bathroom and Madame Charot in the kitchen. You just said so.
Mme Charot I'm out here as well.
Mrs Carrott You're not.
Mr Barrett She's right, Thelma.
Mme Charot I know where I'm supposed to be.
Mrs Carrott You can't stay here.
Mme Charot Well, I'm not budging.
Mrs Carrott But how are you going to come on as Mrs Garrett if you're already here?
Mr Barrett Be reasonable, Thelma.
Mme Charot I'll go as far as the door and no further.
Mrs Carrott (*to the audience*) Bear with us. Thelma, you're in the wrong.
Mme Charot Oh, that's the pot calling the kettle black, isn't it? A minute ago you couldn't even remember what sex you were.
Mrs Carrott Are you going off or do I have to re-cast *Evita*?

Mme Charot considers this

Mme Charot I'll go off this once. Just this once!

Mme Charot exits

Mrs Carrott *(calling out of door D)* Minnie! Minnie!

Mr Parrot enters through door C

Mr Parrot Here are the contracts.

Mrs Carrott Ah, there you are, Mr Parrot. Now don't forget you have to pretend to be Mr Barrett while Monsieur Charot signs the contracts.

Mr Barrett I'll call him in. Monsieur Charot!

Mr Parrot Interrupting. Oh, no, I mustn't read that. Wait, I see these contracts concern the sale of 47, rue de la Postcard.

Mr Barrett That's right. Do you know it?

Mr Parrot I know it well. It's a worthless slum.

Mr Barrett What? You mean Charot's tried to trick me? Give me those contracts. *(He grabs Parrot's script)* Nobody will be signing those today.

He tears up the script and throws the pieces on the floor. Mortified, Parrot crawls about trying to pick them up

Mrs Carrott That was a narrow squeak, sir.

Mr Barrett It certainly was, Mrs Carrott. If it hadn't been for my old friend Parrot, I'd have been in a fine mess. Roger, old son, I don't know what to say.

Mr Parrot *(frantically reading pages)* Nor do I.

Mr Barrett We must celebrate. Go and get your wife and we'll all go out for dinner.

Mr Parrot Are you talking to me?

Mr Barrett Go and get your wife.

Mr Parrot Where is she?

Mr Barrett *(to Mrs Carrott)* Where's his wife?

Mrs Carrott Which one?

Mr Barrett I don't know.

Mr Parrot There was a Mrs Parrot in here on page thirty-one.

Mrs Carrott *(pointing R)* She's out there.

Mr Parrot Well, in that case I'll go and make a cuppa.

Mr Parrot wanders off through door A

Mr Barrett Mrs Carrott, thank goodness this crazy weekend is over.

Thelma as Mrs Norah Garrett, an imperious Northerner, enters through door D

Mrs Garrett Where is my husband?

Mr Barrett Who are you?

Mrs Garrett My name is Norah Garrett and I have reason to believe that my husband, the plumber, is conducting an adulterous liaison in this apartment — (*crying*) — and in the lighting box as well!

Mrs Carrott Thelma, it's not what you think!

Mrs Garrett What do you take me for? I've suspected them for months.

Mrs Carrott Please, Thelma! Joyce is seventy-eight years old. And she's a Virgo. She let that slip at the clinic.

Mrs Garrett It all makes sense now. The surgical stocking in the back of Malcolm's car. The little Sunday trips to the newsagent to get the *Observer*, and then he comes home stinking of liniment ...

Mrs Carrott Let's just remember our gala evening and our friends from across the Channel who are certainly not going to want us to come to the South of France if we don't pull ourselves together, are they, Mrs Garrett?

Mrs Garrett I want to see my husband right this minute.

Mr Barrett He's not here, Mrs Garrett.

Mrs Carrott crosses to the table DR

Mrs Garrett Then you won't mind if I look around?

Mr Barrett Of course not. May I offer you a drink?

Mrs Carrott hurriedly walks backwards to C

Mrs Garrett Thank you. I'll have a port and lemon.

Mr Barrett A port and lemon for Mrs Garrett, Mrs Carrott.

Mrs Carrott Yes, Mr Barrett.

She moves back to the table DR. *Mrs Garrett moves to door C*

Mrs Garrett What's in here?

Mr Barrett This is a perfectly ordinary kitchen.

He opens door C. Mrs Garrett screams

What's the matter?

Mrs Garrett There are three naked people in there.

Barrett checks

Mr Barrett Nudist decorators.

He slams the door. Mrs Garrett screams

Mr Barrett Now what's the matter?

Mrs Garrett You slammed my fingers in the door.

A knock at door D. Mrs Carrott opens it

Mr Barrett My God, who's that?

Mrs Carrott It's Mrs Barrett, your wife, sir.

Mr Barrett My wife! Oh, no! She mustn't catch me alone with two —
(*suppressing laughter*) — young and attractive women. You'll have to
hide.

Mrs Garrett I'm certainly not going to hide.

Mr Barrett Yes, you are. In the cupboard.

*He tries to push her into the cupboard, but it is far too small and he can't get
the door closed*

Mrs Garrett Mr Barrett, stop this at once ...

Mr Barrett Get in.

Mrs Garrett I can't. It's too small.

Mr Barrett Hold the door. I can't shut it.

Mrs Garrett, completely visible, complies

Mrs Garrett Let me out. Let me out.

Barrett grabs Mrs Carrott and they run towards door B

Mr Barrett Quickly, Mrs Carrott. In the bathroom.

Mrs Carrott Mr Barrett, please!

Barrett opens door B. Fifi screams off

Mr Barrett Good lord, the plumber!

He slams the door. Mrs Garrett comes out of the cupboard

Mrs Garrett Did I hear you mention my husband?

Mr Barrett No. Get back in the cupboard.

He pushes her in

Mrs Garrett I'm not staying in this cupb —— Look, it was bigger than this
in rehearsals ...

Mr Barrett It doesn't matter. Hold the door.

Mrs Barrett enters through door D

Mrs Barrett Darling!
Mr Barrett Too early.
Mrs Barrett Sorry.

Mrs Barrett exits

Mr Barrett Quickly, Mrs Carrott. Under this table.

He pulls her down C to where the table used to be

Mrs Carrott What table?
Mr Barrett There should be a table here.

Mrs Garrett comes out of the cupboard

Mrs Garrett I can't breathe in here.
Mr Barrett Stay where you are.

He opens door D revealing:

Mrs Barrett waiting to come on

Mr Barrett Where's the table?
Mrs Barrett What table?
Mr Barrett Doesn't matter.

He closes the door and begins removing everything from the table R

Quickly, Mrs Carrott. Let's get all these things off the table.
Mrs Carrott Gordon, you mustn't touch those props.
Mr Barrett I've got to have something to hide you under. Now just leave
me alone. (*He takes the cloth off the table*)
Mrs Carrott Gordon! Might I remind you ——
Mrs Garrett I can't breathe in here!
Mr Barrett Put this over you. (*He throws a cloth over Mrs Garrett*) Now
get down on the floor. (*To Mrs Carrott*) Why aren't you in the cupboard?
Mrs Carrott I'm not supposed to be in the cupboard.
Mrs Garrett (*removing the cloth*) This should be over *her*.
Mr Barrett Put this over you. (*He throws the cloth over Mrs Carrott*)

Mrs Carrott I've created a monster.
Mr Barrett (*to Mrs Garrett*) Why aren't you in the cupboard?
Mrs Garrett I want to see my husband — (*Crying*)You've got a lot of
explaining to do, Malcolm!

Barrett pushes her back in the cupboard

Mr Barrett Wait for him in here.
Mrs Garrett This is preposterous! Gordon, they can *see* me.
Mr Barrett Don't point at them and they won't see you.
Mrs Garrett Don't you speak to me like that.
Mr Barrett Hold the door.
Mrs Carrott (*removing the cloth*) Why have I got to have this cloth over me,
Gordon?

*Barrett returns to Mrs Carrott, replaces the cloth and makes her kneel on
floor*

Mr Barrett You're going to be an occasional table.
Mrs Carrott Nice idea, Gordon, but I think you're getting a bit carried
away ...

*Barrett moves to open door D, but is forestalled by Mrs Garrett, who comes
out of the cupboard*

Mrs Garrett I've had enough of this.
Mr Barrett Get back in the cupboard.
Mrs Garrett Why should I?

Barrett pushes Mrs Garrett back into the cupboard

Mr Barrett It's just for a few more minutes, Mrs Garrett. Now will you hold
the door?
Mrs Garrett No, I will not hold the door.
Mr Barrett I can't get it closed.

Mrs Carrott gets up and removes the cloth

Mrs Carrott I don't think this is awfully convincing, Gordon ——
Mr Barrett Just keep quiet and remember you're a table.

*Mrs Carrott is on her elbows and knees with the cloth round her shoulders.
Barrett fetches two of the glasses he took from the table*

Mrs Carrott Oh, yes, and then I suppose I'll have to be a yellow washing-up bowl?
Mr Barrett Hold your hands out.
Mrs Carrott (*complying*) What for?

Barrett puts the glasses in her hands

   Gordon!
Mr Barrett What?
Mrs Carrott I feel this table would also have a dish of cashew nuts.

Barrett fetches the dish and places it on her back

Mrs Carrott And a copy of *Vogue*.
Mr Barrett (*shaking his head*) Doesn't work for me.

He moves to the cupboard and leans on it heavily. Mrs Garrett struggles to avoid being squashed

Mrs Carrott (*to the audience*) This man is our stage manager just in case anyone's forgotten ——
Mr Barrett (*interrupting*) Is that you, darling?

   Mrs Barrett enters through door D

Mrs Barrett Darling!
Mr Barrett Darling!
Mrs Barrett I've come to apologize.
Mr Barrett But there's no need.
Mrs Barrett But there is. When I first arrived I foolishly thought you were having a relationship with another woman. But now I can see you have nothing to hide.

Now infuriated, Mrs Garrett bites Barrett's arm

Mr Barrett No, no. I'm here all alone.

Mrs Carrott coughs. Barrett coughs louder

Mrs Barrett Is something the matter?
Mr Barrett My throat's rather dry. I think I need a drink.
Mrs Barrett I'll get you one.
Mr Barrett No, I'll do it. (*He dithers. To Mrs Barrett*) Can you hold the door, please? She won't do a thing I ask her.

Barrett collects a bottle, moves to Mrs Carrott and pours drink into her glasses

Mrs Garrett (*to Mrs Barrett*) And can you wonder at it? Have you heard the way he's been addressing me? And did you know my husband is consorting with a geriatric floozy?

Mrs Barrett Are you pleased to see me, darling?

Mr Barrett Of course I am. (*He returns for the soda syphon*)

Mrs Barrett It's so romantic, isn't it? Just the two of us. All alone.

Mrs Garrett pushes her way out of the cupboard to continue her conversation

Mrs Garrett Does he resent me going out, is that what it is? I leave his meals in the oven——

Seeing Mrs Garrett out of the cupboard, Gordon accidentally squirts soda into Mrs Carrott's face

Mrs Carrott Gordon!

Mrs Barrett I think I'll freshen up.

Mr Barrett You can't.

Mrs Barrett Why not?

Mr Barrett The bathroom door's jammed.

Mrs Barrett But I was going to the kitchen.

Mr Barrett You can't go in there either.

Mrs Barrett Why?

Mr Barrett Em ...

Mrs Garrett (*crying*) It's being decorated.

Mr Barrett Yes, it's being decorated.

Mrs Barrett Well, where *can* I go?

Mr Barrett (*to Mrs Carrott*) Where can she go?

Mrs Carrott Bathroom in the foyer.

Mr Barrett That's right.

He propels Mrs Barrett out of door D

Mrs Barrett Who am I next?

Mr Barrett I don't know.

While Mrs Garrett is talking, Mr Barrett opens door B and takes out a lampshade

Mrs Garrett Look at her up there with the two top buttons of her cardigan undone! Would she dress like that for the Meals on Wheels lady? I think not.

Barrett puts the lampshade on Mrs Garrett's head, then opens door C revealing:

Minnie eating a banana

Mr Barrett Who are you?
Minnie I help with the costumes.
Mr Barrett (*to Mrs Carrott*) Who is she?
Mrs Carrott Roger Parrot.
Mr Barrett Come out of there, Parrot.
Minnie I thought I'd finished.

Barrett takes an empty picture frame from behind the bed and gets Minnie to hold it in front of herself

Mr Barrett My wife mustn't find you here. Now hold that and pretend you're *The Laughing Cavalier*.
Minnie I ought to be keeping an eye on the tea urn really.

Barrett collects Mrs Carrott and bundles her out of door D

Mr Barrett Quickly, Mrs Carrott. In the foyer.
Mrs Carrott Find Minnie another script.
Mr Barrett I haven't got time.

Mrs Carrott exits through door D. Barrett exits through door C. Mrs Barrett enters through door D

Mrs Barrett Well, that was most refreshing. Hmmm, I don't remember that hideous painting. Or that ghastly lamp standard come to that. And where is my husband?

Barrett enters through door C

Mr Barrett Here I am, darling. I've just been whipping up a devil's food cake in the kitchen.
Mrs Barrett But isn't it being decorated?
Mr Barrett Of course it is. Lemon icing and glacé cherries. Now come over here. I want to look at you.
Mrs Barrett It's impossible to see anything in this light. I'll turn on the standard lamp.
Mr Barrett No!
Mrs Barrett Why not?

Mr Barrett It's broken. In fact I'm just going to take it away to have it repaired. Have you noticed that very interesting portrait?

Mrs Barrett Yes. What is it?

Mr Barrett *The Laughing Cavalier.*

Mrs Barrett It doesn't look like it.

Mr Barrett Sorry. "The Laughing Cavalier's Next Door Neighbour". That's what I meant to say.

Mrs Barrett examines Minnie, who offers her a bite of her banana. Barrett tries to lift Mrs Garrett

Mrs Garrett What do you think you're doing?

Mr Barrett My wife's beginning to suspect. You'll have to hide in the kitchen.

He pushes her through door C

Mrs Garrett exits

Mrs Barrett Who were you talking to, darling?

Mr Barrett Myself. I've been under a bit of stress recently. My business partner, Monsieur Charot, tried to sell me a slum.

Mrs Barrett Oh!

Pause

Mr Barrett Yes.

Mrs Barrett Who can that be knocking at the door ... so impatiently?

Mr Barrett I'll go and see.

He moves to door D and opens it revealing no-one

Monsieur Charot! (*He looks out*) Is that you, Monsieur Charot, coming to explain everything?

Mrs Reece is glimpsed in the doorway

What shall we do?

Mrs Reece You want me to sort things out, do you? You don't want me to be a chest of drawers or anything like that?

Mr Barrett I don't know where I went wrong, Mrs Reece.

Mrs Reece It's not as easy as it looks, you see.

She disappears

Mrs Barrett stands in front of Minnie and tries to push her towards door C

Mrs Barrett You've got to come on as Monsieur Charot.
Minnie I haven't got to say anything, have I?
Mrs Barrett Just get out here. Come in the other door.
Minnie But I've got the tea on.

Mrs Barrett pushes Minnie through door C and slams it

   Minnie exits

Mrs Barrett So, Monsieur Charot: you're the man who tried to defraud my
   husband?

Mrs Reece appears, scribbling on a piece of paper, in the open doorway D

Mrs Reece No, forget that.
Mr Barrett (*to Mrs Barrett*) I was wrong. Monsieur Charot isn't here.

Mrs Reece hands Barrett the paper and ducks out of sight

Mr Barrett (*reading*) "In fact he's dead. He's fallen in front of a bus."

Minnie enters through door D, still holding the picture frame

Mr Barrett Who are you?
Minnie Monsieur Charot.

Barrett screws up the note in exasperation

Mrs Barrett What have you got to say for yourself?
Minnie (*after some consideration*) Do you take one lump or two?

Mrs Reece waves another script through door D

Minnie takes it, handing the picture frame to Mrs Barrett

Minnie Where is Monsieur Barrett?
Mr Barrett Why do you want to know?
Minnie By mistake I gave him the wrong contracts. Here are the correct ones.
Mr Barrett Let me see.

*He snatches Minnie's script. Fearing the worst, Minnie snatches it back
again. Barrett reads over Minnie's shoulder*

Ah, yes. This is more like it. The property for sale is the highly desirable residence at 44, rue de l'Amour.

Mrs Garrett bursts in through door C

Mrs Garrett 44, rue de l'Amour? How dare you try and sell our holiday home? (*She whips the script out of Minnie's hands and tears it up*) Perhaps you'd like to tell me what you're doing here, how those contracts came to be in your possession, why you're trying to sell property that doesn't belong to you — (*crying*) — and where I can get a good divorce lawyer ...?

Minnie looks out of door D

Minnie Have you got any more scripts?

Mrs Reece appears

Mrs Reece Who are you?
Minnie Monsieur Charot.
Mrs Reece You're dead.
Minnie Sorry, Thelma, I'm dead.
Mrs Garrett I wish I were dead! I've got nothing else to live for ...!
Mrs Reece Thelma! (*Pause*) Button it.
Mrs Garrett What ...?
Mrs Reece Somebody left the tea urn on. It's boiling over.

Mrs Reece exits

Minnie Oh, that was me. I'll come and turn it off.
Mrs Barrett Minnie, stay where you are.
Minnie But I'm dead.
Mrs Barrett You're ruining this play...*all* of you!
Minnie There'll be an explosion, Felicity...
Mr Barrett I'll go.

Mr Barrett exits through door D

Minnie Can you put it on number two, Gordon? Then it'll be ready when we come off ——
Mrs Barrett (*interrupting*) Will somebody please tell me what's going on?
Mrs Garrett We've narrowly escaped being swindled by a confidence trickster.
Mrs Barrett How awful. But at least my husband and I can now relax and enjoy our weekend in Paris.

Mrs Garrett And I can have that port and lemon.

Mrs Barrett screams and points at spot DC where table used to be

Mrs Barrett Why is that ... table moving?

There is a clattering behind door D. Mrs Barrett returns the picture frame to Minnie and opens the door

The table enters with Mrs Reece and Gordon under it. They place it DC

Mrs Barrett Is somebody under that table?
Minnie Mrs Reece.
Mrs Barrett Ssshh!

Mrs Reece emerges from beneath the table

Mrs Reece No, there's nobody under the table.
Mrs Barrett Who are you?
Mrs Reece I'd have preferred advance warning of that question.
Mrs Barrett Where is my husband?
Mrs Reece Give me a moment.
Mrs Barrett (*to Mrs Garrett*) Do you know where he is?
Mrs Garrett I don't even know who he is.
Minnie I know who he is.
Mrs Barrett Who?
Minnie You.
Mrs Barrett No, I'm not my husband, Minnie.
Mrs Reece Well, I'm sure that, whoever your husband is, Mrs Barrett, he
    must be somewhere. Hark! I think I can hear someone coming down the
    corridor. I'll just go and see who it is.

Mrs Reece exits through door D

Everyone is left bewildered as to what might happen next

Mrs Barrett (*to Minnie*) Say you're my husband.
Minnie What?
Mrs Garrett Don't start that again!
Mrs Barrett *Pretend* you're my husband.
Minnie Shall I still hold the picture frame?
Mrs Barrett Well, if it isn't my husband!

*Mrs Reece enters through door D wearing Mr Carrott's blazer over Mrs
Carrott's dress*

Mrs Reece Well, if it isn't my wife! Excuse my appearance, darling, but I got caught in a sudden downpour and my secretary lent me her frock.

Mrs Barrett (*indicating Minnie*) But this is my husband.

Mrs Reece Oh, he was here all along, was he? I meant to say, of course, that I'm your ex-husband, aren't I?

Mrs Barrett Yes.

Barrett emerges from beneath the table

Mr Barrett No, hang on a sec. I think I'm her husband. Sorry.

Mrs Reece Oh, you've gone completely to pieces now, haven't you, Gordon? Where are you supposed to be, dear?

Mr Barrett Don't know.

Mrs Reece Never mind. We'll work it out. Any suggestions, folk? Thelma?

Mrs Garrett I don't honestly care, Phoebe.

Mrs Reece Come along, dear. Where do you think Gordon ought to be?

Mrs Garrett A mental home.

Mrs Reece You've got to get a grip on yourself, dear.

Mrs Garrett (*increasingly hysterical*) My life is in ruins, Phoebe. As soon as the curtain comes down, I'm going to take slow poison. Now please don't expect me to know whether or not our stage manager should be in the bathroom!

Mrs Garrett slumps on the bed, which collapses again. She thrashes about, wielding the pillow and bleating for some moments. Finally she has come to an exhausted stop

Mrs Reece Has something upset you, dear?

Mrs Garrett moans in frustration

(*To the audience*) This won't take a moment. Thelma, it's true. Joyce has been having secret meetings with Malcolm.

Mrs Garrett I'm not a fool, Phoebe.

Mrs Reece They've been planning a surprise birthday party for you, dear.

Mrs Garrett My birthday was last week.

Mrs Reece Did you have a party?

Mrs Garrett No.

Mrs Reece That was the surprise.

Mrs Garrett I'm going home. Malcolm, switch these lights out.

Black-out

Mrs Reece Malcolm, we can't do the finale in the dark. Now turn the lights on again immediately. We're waiting, Malcolm. Malcolm, are you still up there? Oh, dear. Well, I'm afraid that appears to be the end of the play, ladies and gentlemen. Can you find your way to the exit doors, do you think? Those with cigarette lighters could be team leaders. Mesdames et monsieurs, la comédie est finie. And naturally Thelma Greenwood's first-class air tickets to the South of France will be returned to you on your way out.

Thelma (*off*) All right, I'll do the finale! Turn the bloody lights back on!

The Lights come up revealing Minnie and Gordon casually drinking tea. They guiltily put the mugs behind their backs

Mrs Reece Voilà! Well, we've certainly had a hectic time in Paris, haven't we? Life will seem très ordinaire back in [*name of town*]. But there's a couple of hours before the Hovercraft leaves.

Gordon Does that mean...?

Mrs Reece Yes! Let's all go to the Moulin Rouge!

Whoops as everyone dashes off

Black-out. The Lights around the top of the flats are illuminated. Music: the Cancan from Orpheus in the Underworld. *The Lights come up to full*

Gordon, with gendarme's cap and whistle, chases on the others, in cancan frills. Somebody brings on and sets a model of the Eiffel Tower

After a chase routine, everyone converges c and dances. There are feeble attempts at a cartwheel, the splits, hopping with the other leg held aloft, etc. Finally the four women assist Gordon in performing a backflip. The Eiffel Tower lights up

CURTAIN

FURNITURE AND PROPERTY LIST

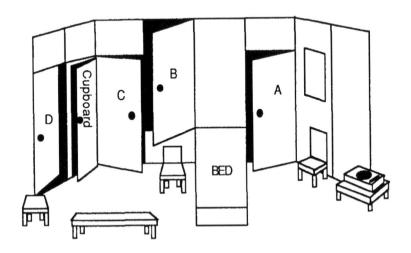

PROLOGUE

On stage: Bed. On it: pillow, bedclothes
Table DL. *On it*: record player, half-filled bottle of milk. *By it*: 2
LPs
Table DR. *On it*: cloth, dish of nuts, drinks, soda syphon, glasses,
telephone, notepad, pencil
Table C
2 upright chairs

Off stage: Tricolours (**Mrs Reece, Thelma**)
Hoover (**Fifi**)
Plate of sandwiches (**Gordon**)
Stick of make-up (**Thelma**)

Personal: **Mrs Reece**: handbag

ACT I

On stage: As before

Off stage: Pencil (**Gordon**)
Script (**Mr Parrot**)
Piece of paper (**Gordon**)
Ball and skein of knitting wool, knitting pattern for **Mr Parrot**
     (**Stage Management**)
Briefcase (**Mrs Carrott**)
Sheaf of papers (**Stage Management**)
Suitcases (**Mr Carrott**)

Personal: **Fifi**: bandage on leg, duster
Mr Parrot: spectacles, moustache (worn throughout), pin
     cushion on wrist, sewing needle with thread in lapel, 2
     cigarettes in top pocket
Mrs Barrett: handbag containing various contents

ENTR'ACTE

Re-set: Bed

Set: Small table c. *On it*: mixing bowl, false egg, bag of flour, hand
     whisk with detachable handle

Off stage: Small apron (**Mrs Reece**)
Plate with tinfoil-covered squashed sponge (**Thelma**)

Personal: **Thelma**: tricolour

ACT II

Set: Empty picture frame behind bed

Off stage: Hoover (**Fifi**)
Toolbag (**Thelma**)
2 saucepan lids (**Thelma**)
Washboard (**Gordon**)

Spoons (**Minnie**)
Lampshade (**Stage Management**)
Banana (**Minnie**)
Pencil, piece of paper (**Mrs Reece**)
Script (**Mrs Reece**)
2 mugs of tea (**Stage Management**)
Eiffel Tower model (**Cast member**)

Personal: **Mr Parrot**: handkerchief, eyebrow pencil in pocket
Jojo: string of onions round neck
Gordon: gendarme's whistle
Thelma: tricolour

LIGHTING PLOT

Practical fittings required: lights around the top of the flats; Eiffel Tower model

PROLOGUE

To open: General half-lighting; House Lights on

Cue 1	**Felicity** takes the Hoover and exits through door D	(Page 3)
	House lights down	
Cue 2	**Mrs Reece** backs through door D	(Page 7)
	Fade to black-out	

ACT I

To open: Full lighting on area R

Cue 3	**Parrot** exits	(Page 13)
	Crossfade to L	
Cue 4	**Mme Charot** leads **Mr Parrot** out	(Page 17)
	Bring up full lighting	
Cue 5	**Mme Charot**: "Embrassé-moi, mon imbécile!"	(Page 20)
	Black-out	
Cue 6	**Mme Charot**: " ... playing at up there?"	(Page 20)
	Bring up full lighting	
Cue 7	**Fifi**: "And over 'ere ..."	(Page 21)
	Black-out. When ready bring up lighting L	
Cue 8	**Fifi**: "You freeze!"	(Page 22)
	Crossfade to R	

Cue 9	**Mr Barrett**: " ... come out of this bathroom."	(Page 23)
	Crossfade to L	
Cue 10	**Mrs Carrott** and **Mr Barrett** shuffle out	(Page 27)
	Crossfade to R	
Cue 11	**Mme Charot** moves to take off the nightie	(Page 29)
	Black-out. When ready bring up lighting L	
Cue 12	The window flat collapses	(Page 30)
	Black-out. Bring up house lights	

ENTR'ACTE

To open: House Lights on, spot on **Mrs Reece**

Cue 13	**Thelma** and **Mrs Reece** exit	(Page 34)
	Black-out	

ACT II

To open: Full general lighting

Cue 14	**Mrs Garrett**: "Malcolm, switch these lights out."	(Page 54)
	Black-out	
Cue 15	**Thelma**: "Turn the bloody lights back on!"	(Page 55)
	Bring up full general lighting	
Cue 16	Everyone dashes off	(Page 55)
	Black-out. Bring up lights around the top of the flats; bring up full general lighting	
Cue 17	**Gordon** performs a backflip	(Page 55)
	Eiffel Tower model lights up	

EFFECTS PLOT

Please note that a licence issued by Samuel French Ltd to perform this play does not include permission to use the Overture and Incidental music specified in this copy. Where the place of performance is already licensed by the PERFORMING RIGHT SOCIETY a return of the music used must be made to them. If the place of performance is not so licensed then application should be made to the Performing Right Society, 29 Berners Street, London W1.

A separate and additional licence from PHONOGRAPHIC PERFORMANCES LTD, Ganton House, Ganton Street, London W1 is needed whenever commercial recordings are used.

PROLOGUE

Cue 1   To open   (Page 1)
           Music: Offenbach's Orpheus in the Underworld

Cue 2   When ready   (Page 1)
           Cut music; begin Hoover effect and telephone ringing

Cue 3   **Fifi** switches off the Hoover   (Page 1)
           Cut Hoover effect

Cue 4   **Fifi** picks up the telephone receiver   (Page 1)
           Cut telephone

Cue 5   **Fifi** switches on the Hoover   (Page 2)
           Hoover effect with telephone ringing

Cue 6   **Fifi** picks up the telephone receiver   (Page 2)
           Cut telephone

Cue 7   **Mrs Reece:** " ... turn that tape recorder off?"   (Page 2)
           Cut Hoover effect

Cue 8   **Fifi** switches on the Hoover   (Page 4)
           Hoover effect

Cue 9	**Mrs Reece**: " ... Hoovered to death down here."	(Page 4)
	Cut Hoover effect	
Cue 10	**Mrs Reece** exits uncertainly	(Page 5)
	Burst of Hoover effect; cut abruptly	
Cue 11	**Fifi** kicks the socket	(Page 5)
	Flash	

ACT I

Cue 12	**Fifi** switches on the Hoover. Pause	(Page 8)
	Hoover effect, telephone rings	
Cue 13	**Fifi** answers the telephone	(Page 8)
	Cut telephone	
Cue 14	**Fifi** takes a step towards the Hoover	(Page 8)
	Cut Hoover effect	
Cue 15	**Fifi** pulls out a duster	(Page 9)
	Hoover effect	
Cue 16	**Fifi** stands up as if surprised	(Page 10)
	Cut Hoover effect	
Cue 17	**Mme Charot**: "It begins very quietly."	(Page 11)
	Hoover effect briefly	
Cue 18	**Mme Charot**: " ... ze ozair side."	(Page 15)
	Recording of Stevie Wonder briefly	
Cue 19	**Mr Parrot**: " ... walked off with it ..."	(Page 15)
	Recording of Offenbach's Apache Dance	
Cue 20	**Mrs Carrott**: "Ssshh."	(Page 22)
	Hoover effect momentarily	
Cue 21	Black-out	(Page 31)
	Hoover effect followed by recording of Orpheus in the Underworld	

ENTR'ACTE

No cues

ACT II

Cue 22   To open   (Page 35)
            Hoover effect

Cue 23   **Fifi** begins cleaning   (Page 35)
            Telephone

Cue 24   **Fifi** stops cleaning   (Page 35)
            Cut Hoover effect

Cue 25   **Fifi** picks up the receiver   (Page 35)
            Cut telephone

Cue 26   **Fifi** hangs up   (Page 35)
            Hoover effect

Cue 27   **Mrs Garrett**: "Joyce!"   (Page 35)
            Cut Hoover effect

Cue 28   The Lights around the top of the flats are illuminated (Page 55)
            Music: the Cancan from Orpheus in the Underworld

Lightning Source UK Ltd.
Milton Keynes UK
UKOW06f1944050517
300619UK00014B/277/P